D1451954

Written By:
Miquilaue Young

Mama Says

Homebirth

Illustrated By: Chase P. Walker
Designed By: MyGoose Media

MyGoose
MEDIA

In Memory of
Grandma Mattie Lee Davis

ISBN 978-0-578-62849-3
Library of Congress Control Number: 2019921215

First printing edition 20

Miquilaue Young
Ferguson, MO
www.youngsurrender.com

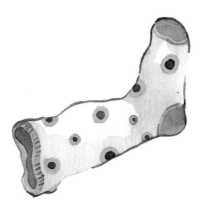
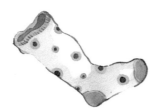

Written By:
Miquilaue Young

Mama Says

Homebirth

Illustrated By: Chase P. Walker

Mama says my Gran-Gran and Grandma were born at home by a midwife, just like me! Mama says all my great aunties and uncles were born at home in West Memphis, Arkansas in the same house with a midwife.

2

Mama says there is a legacy of homebirths in our family.

4

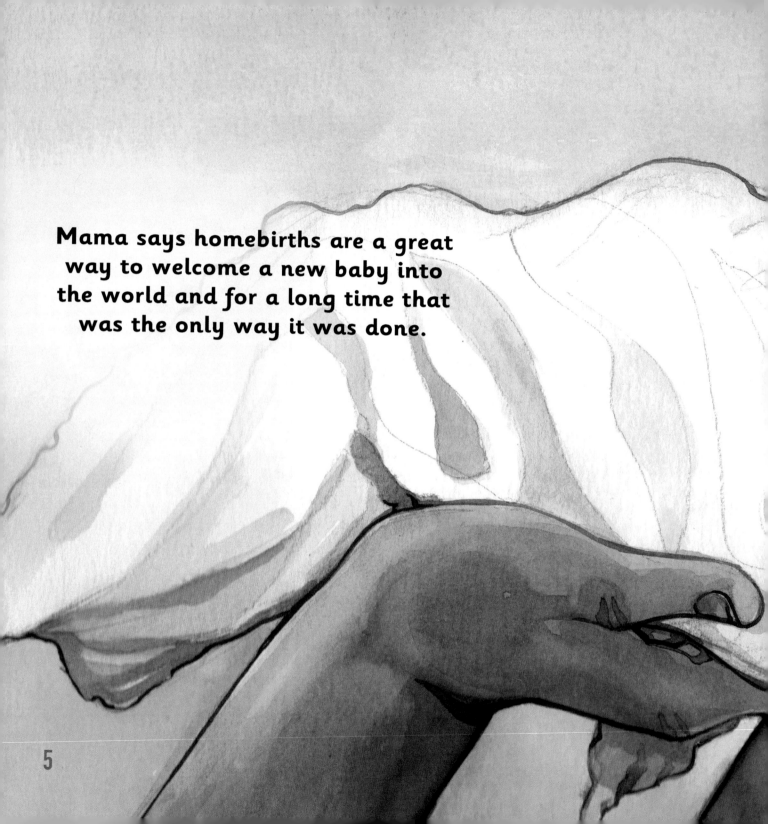

Mama says homebirths are a great way to welcome a new baby into the world and for a long time that was the only way it was done.

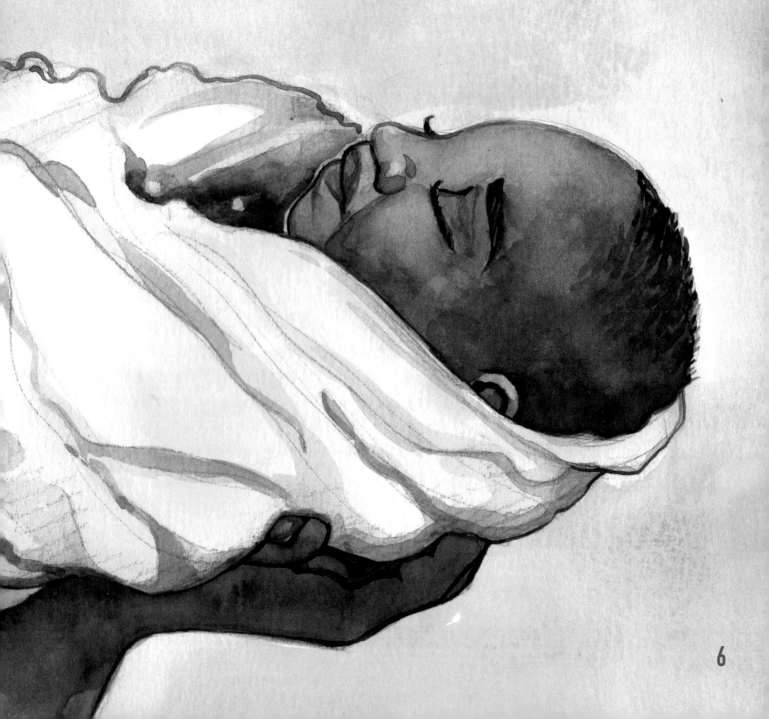

Mama says her body was
created to have babies
naturally and even though
that sounds scary, it's not.

Mama says she just breathes, believes, relaxes and lets her body do its' job.

10

Mama says when she and daddy first found out they were going to have me, they met with their midwife every month, but at the end they saw her more often.

11

Mama says the midwife uses special tools to listen to the baby's heartbeat and she measures mama's belly to make sure the baby is growing okay.

14

Mama says there's just something
special about midwives. They take
such good care of mommies and
their babies when they're helping
them to be born.

16

17

Mama says one day when she feels her tummy get tight and hard as a rock and she feels some pains like a tummy ache, she knows it's almost time for the new baby to come.

Mama says her midwife is her coach,
cheerleader, and friend all rolled into one.

20

Mama says that her midwife, along with grandma and daddy make a great team when she's about to have a baby.

22

Mama says that her midwife and daddy know just what she needs without her having to say a word. That's important when a mama is having a baby.

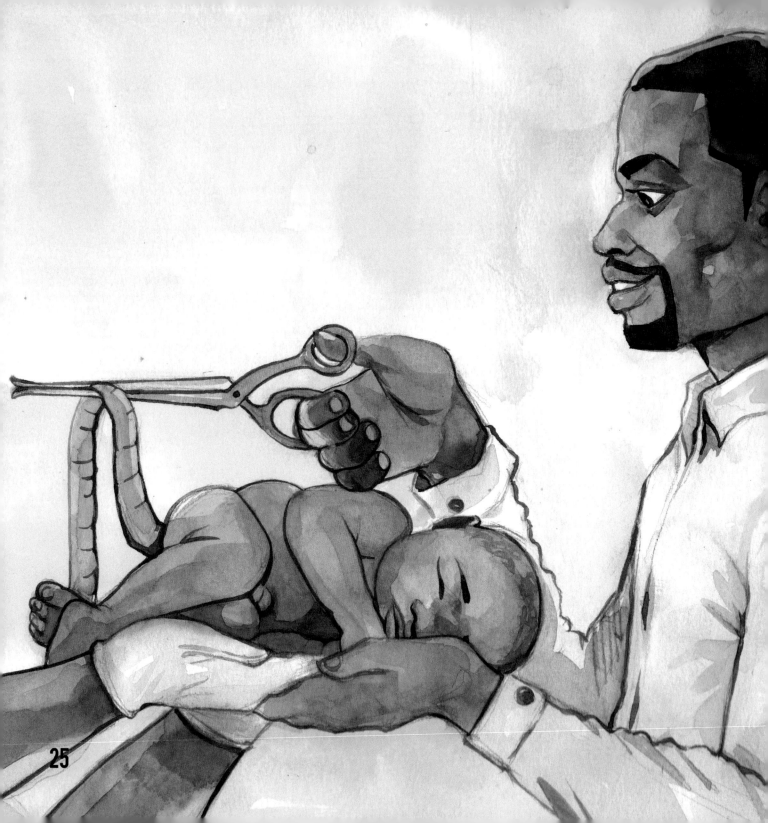

Mama says it's our family's tradition that daddy cuts the cord and gets the new baby dressed.

26

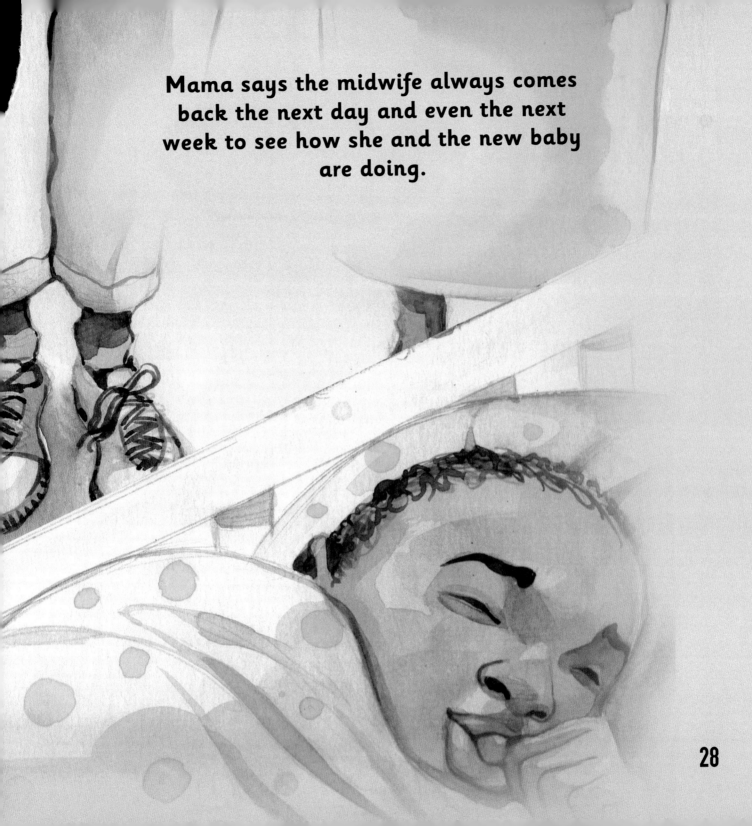

Mama says the midwife always comes back the next day and even the next week to see how she and the new baby are doing.

28

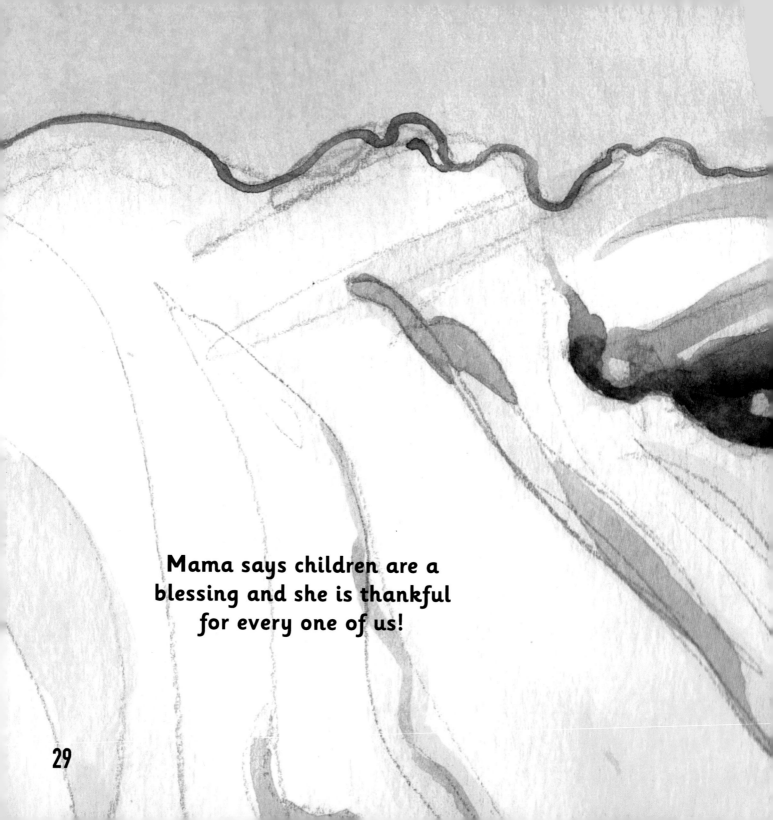

Mama says children are a
blessing and she is thankful
for every one of us!

29

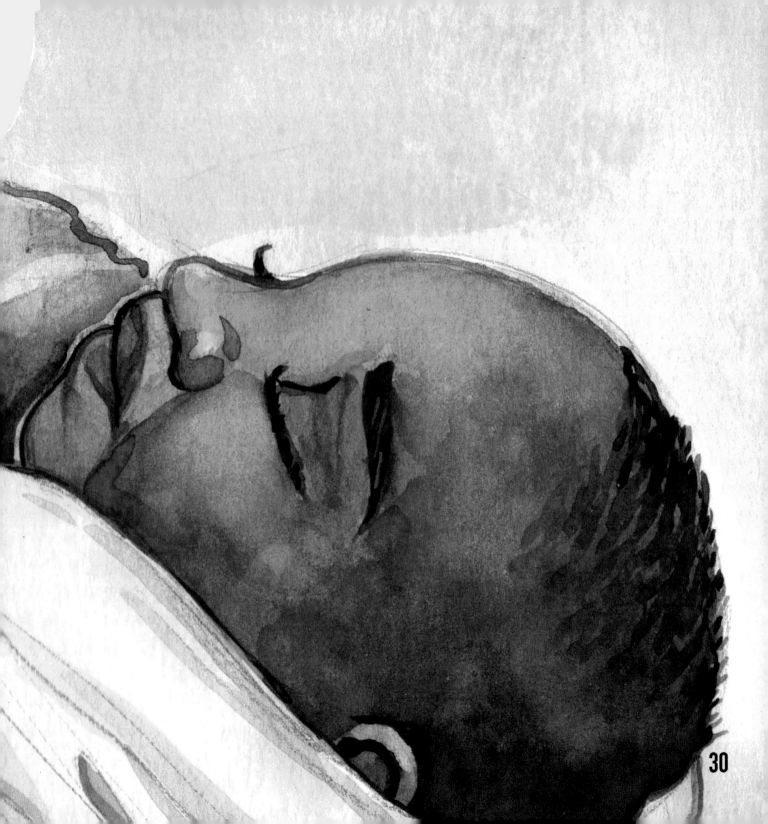

30

Made in the USA
Middletown, DE
05 December 2020